TOKIO HOTEL FEVER

Copyright © ECW Press, 2010
Published by ECW Press, 2120 Queen Street East, Suite 200, Toronto, Ontario, Canada M4E 1E2
416.694.3348 / info@ecwpress.com

Originally published by Michel Lafon. ISBN: 978-2-7499-0869-4.
Copyright © Michel Lafon Publishing S.A., 2007

Library and Archives Canada Cataloguing in Publication

Nouveau, Béatrice
Tokio Hotel fever / Béatrice Nouveau.

Translation of: Tokio Hotel: le tsunami.
ISBN 978-1-55022-928-8

1. Tokio Hotel (Musical group). 2. Rock musicians—Germany. I. Title.

ML421.T62N93 2010   782.42166092'2   C2009-905961-4

French edition edited by Marie Dreyfuss; design and production by Pierre Gay and Matheiu Thauvin

Special thanks to Universal Music Group, for their support of young talent; David Nouveau and his invaluable direction in documenting teenagers;
Sophie Debray-Moreau, for her input and help; and all the fantastic staff of Michel Lafon Publishing . . . and Gilles Lhote.

Translated by Jeanne Duperreault
Edited and additional text by Crissy Boylan
Printing: Shanghai Chenxi Printing   1   2   3   4   5

Photo Credits
Cover: © Abaca - © R. Corlouer
Interior: *Visual*: p.6, 23, 24, 42 (x3), 46 (bottom), 47 (right), 50 (right), 54 (top), 69 (bottom), 112. *Sipa*: p.8–9, 10–11, 14–15, 16–17, 20, 21, 43 (right), 51 (bottom), 55 (bottom), 56–57, 58–59, 62–63, 64 (x2), 66–67, 68 (x2), 69 (top), 71 (x2), 72–73 (x3), 74–75, 82–83, 86 (x3), 96, 97, 88, 89 (x3), 93, 94–95, 110, 111. *Starface*: p. 34–35, 36–37, 43 (top left), 76, 77 (x4), 78 (x2), 79 (x2), 80, 81, 88, 89, 90, 91, 92. *Renaud Corlouer*: p. 38–39, 40, 43 (bottom), 44, 46 (top), 48, 50 (bottom), 51 (left), 52, 54 (bottom), 55 (top), 100, 102, 105, 106 (x2), 107 (x2). *Abaca*: p. 12–13, 32–33, 42 (middle), 47 (left), 60–61, 71 (top), 84, 85, 86 (x3), 87, 88 (x2), 89, 92, 108. *DR*: p. 18–19, 26–27, 28–29, 30–31, 55 (top), 66 (framed), 108 (x4), 111 (x2). *Christina Radish/Agency Photos*: 96 (top). *AP Images/Johannes Eisele Pool*: 98. *AP Images/Evan Agostini/Picture Group*: 99.

Printed and Bound in China

Béatrice Nouveau

ECW Press

TOKIO HOTEL FEVER

The Tokio Hotel fever is infecting the planet, after sweeping across Europe. It's a phenomenon that no music industry insider predicted, and for good reason: there's nothing obvious that makes these rockers stand out from so many other current groups. What makes them different? There are four of them like the Beatles, The Who, Led Zeppelin, System of a Down, and Metallica. They were friends growing up together, like many popular groups. Bill and Tom are brothers, as are the Youngs of AC/DC and the Gallaghers of Oasis. What's more, they're twins — just like the Bee Gees, The Proclaimers, and Good Charlotte. So, what does Tokio Hotel have that is so special?

Simply, their identity. These young men from Magdeburg, Germany, have learned how to express their music, their style, their lyrics . . . in their own language. And then they went on to captivate non-German speaking countries. That is their strength and their greatest talent. Not so long ago, German rock with an edge of electro-punk, such as Tangerine Dream, Faust, or Can, was scorned and labeled "krautrock" or "sauerkraut rock." Most people would agree that German is not the most melodious language. Even Mozart admitted it. But Tokio Hotel has combined the formality of their native tongue with their own sound, which is both supple and powerful, and further softened by the young-sounding voice of the very androgynous Bill.

Captivated by Tokio Hotel's lyrics, the public was soon won over and the band bid *Auf Wiedersehen* to empty German concert halls. They use simple words, from the heart, that deal with adolescent anxieties: love, sex, breaking up, suicide . . . universal themes that cross all barriers. That is another reason for the group's success: everyone can identify with these four young musicians. They speak directly to a whole generation of teenagers, who feel alone and misunderstood as they start off in life. At the age of 24, a young German named Goethe wrote *The Sorrows of Young Werther*, which would initiate a feverish wave of Romanticism across Europe. And he confided, "The effect of this small book was huge, even monstrous, particularly because it happened just at the right time." Tokio Hotel has hit at just the right moment and are poised to enter the realm of legend. . . .

HUNGRY FOR THE SPOTLIGHT

« We were meant to be onstage. That's where everything started for us.

The ultimate dream would be to give concerts all over the world. We have the most fun when we're playing for an audience.

Bill

Sold out! Like international stars, it takes Tokio Hotel only a few hours to sell out the largest concert halls. Tokio Hotel has conquered Europe and is preparing to take over the rest of the world. Shown here in Hamburg, on October 21, 2006, at a gala celebrating 50 years of Bravo magazine.

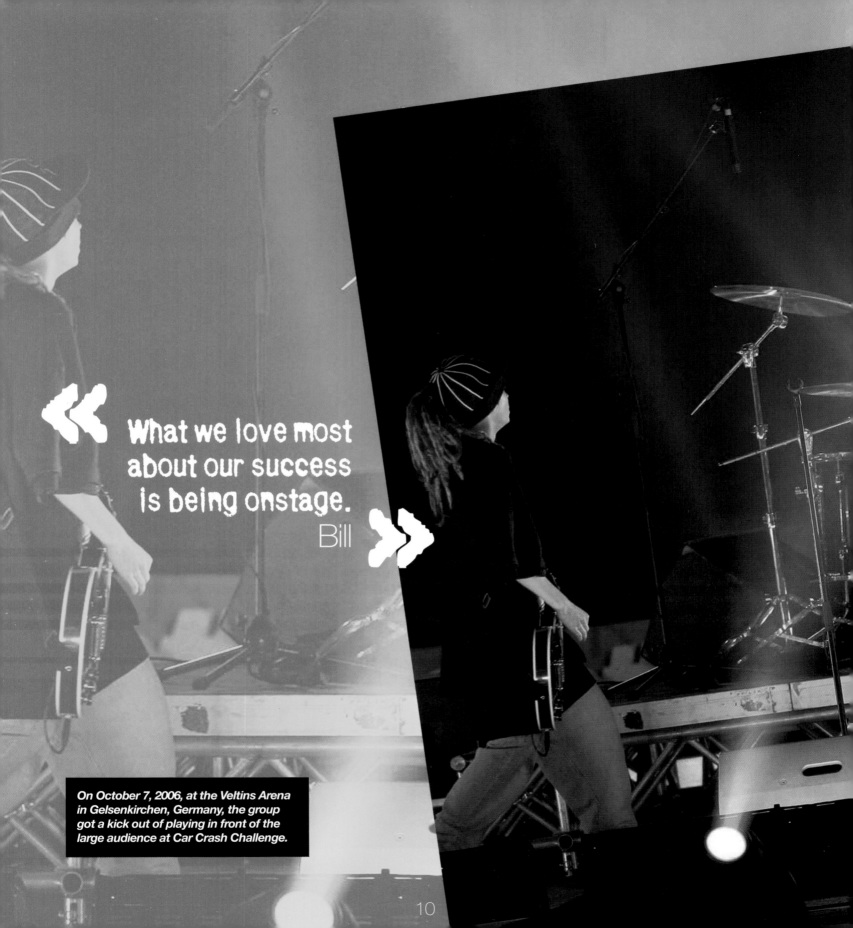

« **What we love most about our success is being onstage.**

Bill »

On October 7, 2006, at the Veltins Arena in Gelsenkirchen, Germany, the group got a kick out of playing in front of the large audience at Car Crash Challenge.

I can easily see the front rows in the smaller venues, and I love having that visual contact with the audience.
Bill

12

An emotional moment during Tokio Hotel's May 1, 2007, performance in front of thousands of fans at the Colorline Arena in their hometown of Hamburg.

A special moment of musical collaboration between the Kaulitz twins onstage at the Munich Olympiahalle, April 24, 2007.

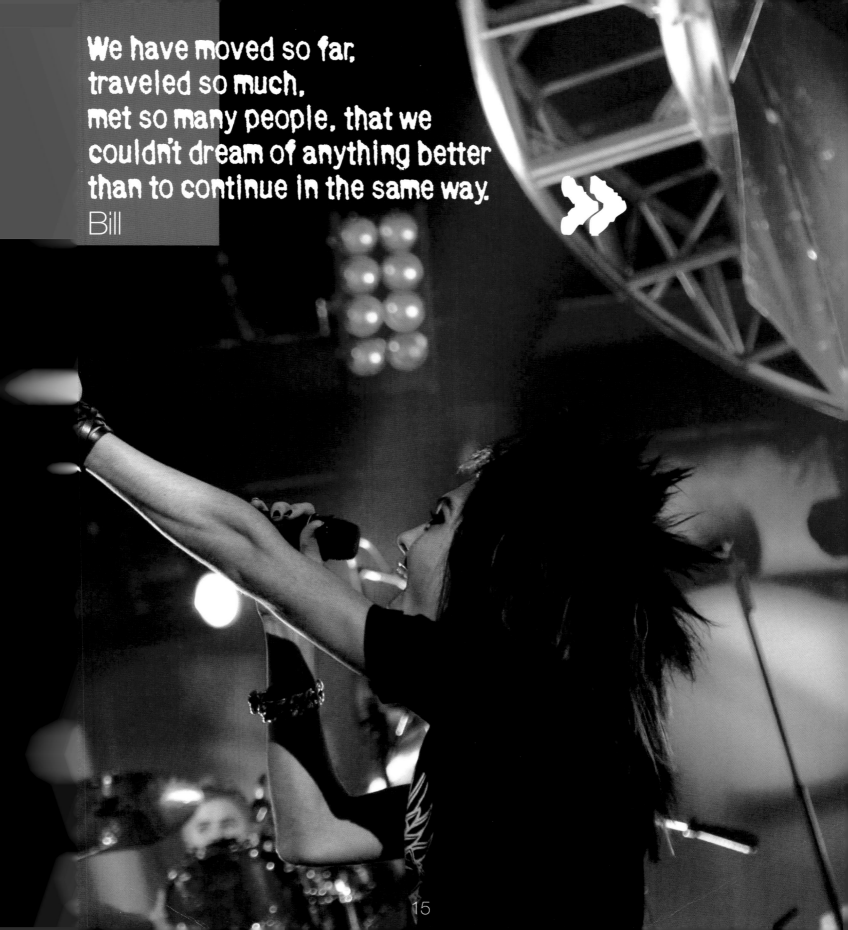

We have moved so far,
traveled so much,
met so many people, that we
couldn't dream of anything better
than to continue in the same way.
Bill

15

Georg blazes beside Bill for the audience at Dôme 41 in Mannheim, March 2, 2007.

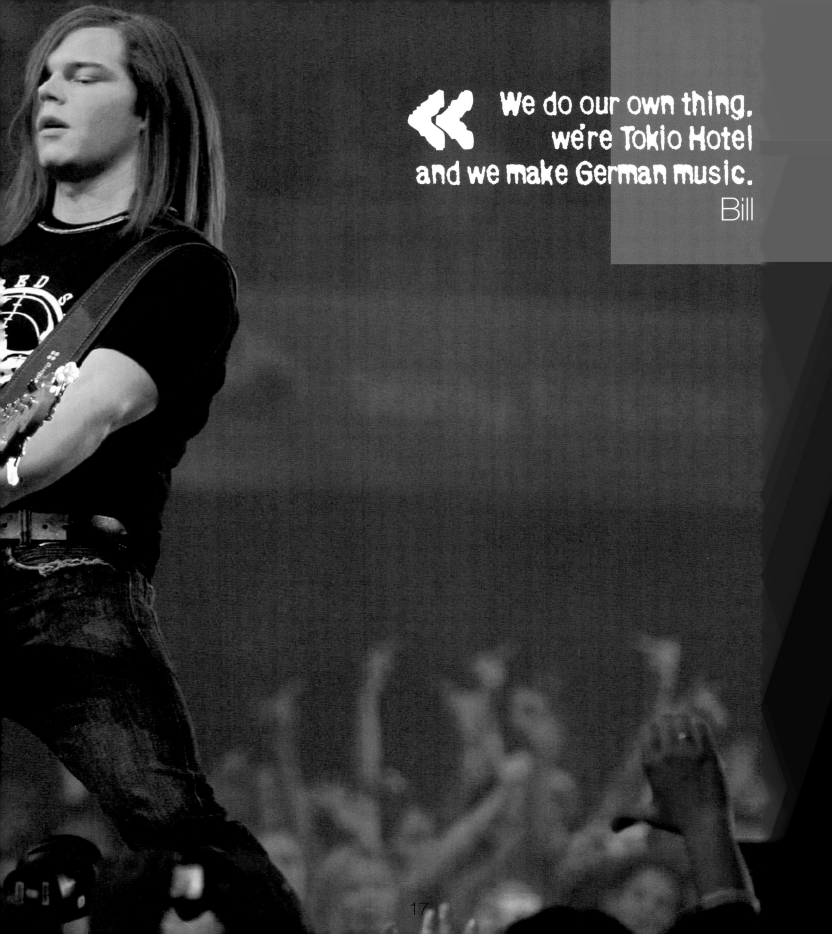

**◀◀ We do our own thing,
we're Tokio Hotel
and we make German music.**
Bill

Whenever TH lets go onstage, hysteria ensues. The crowd goes wild and starts to sing along with Bill. German becomes the universal language of the night!

The fans often bring funny posters they've made. One begged, 'Tom, drop your guitar and come with me.'
Tom

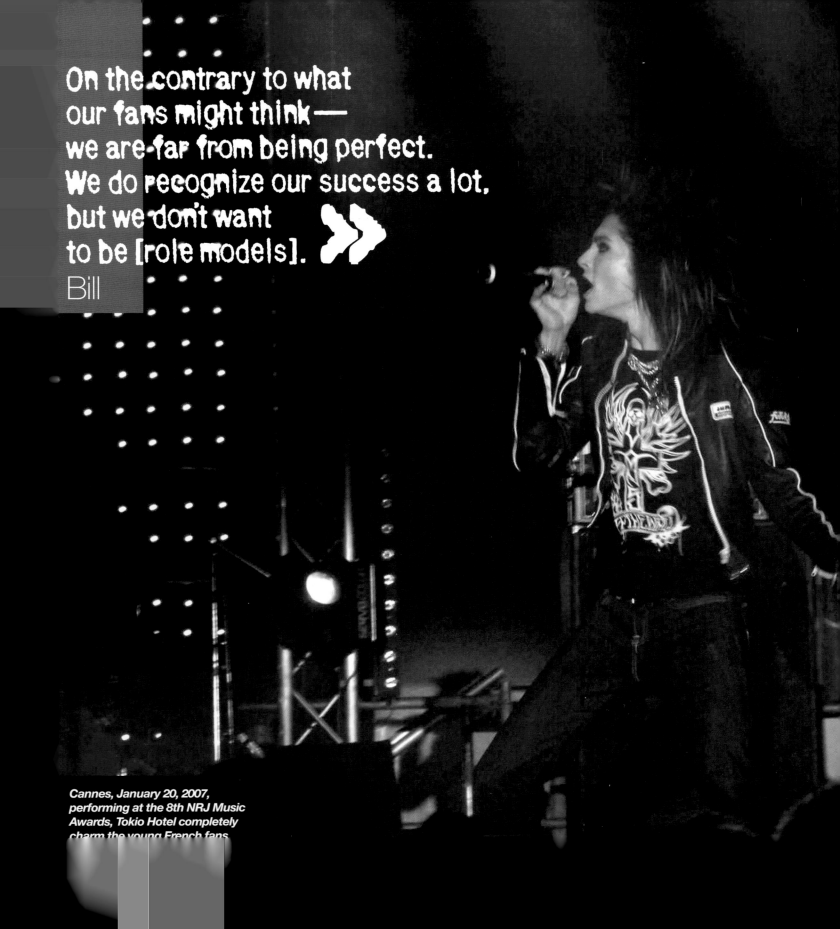

On the contrary to what
our fans might think—
we are far from being perfect.
We do recognize our success a lot,
but we don't want
to be [role models].
Bill

Cannes, January 20, 2007,
performing at the 8th NRJ Music
Awards, Tokio Hotel completely
charm the young French fans.

A competition for 10- to 15-year-olds, the German TV show Kinder-Star-Search showcased a future star when 13-year-old Bill Kaulitz took to the stage. Despite trying his best, he only reached second place, performing the song "It's Raining Men," originally recorded by the Weather Girls and covered by Geri Halliwell in 2001.

"When I was small, I said that I would be a musician when I grew up. Nobody believed me and thought that I would eventually find something else to do. But look at me! You could never imagine me as a lawyer or a banker. That would be ridiculous!" Bill

Germany, 1989

A little more than two months before the fall of the Berlin Wall, Tom and Bill Kaulitz came into the world (in that order, about 10 minutes apart). They were born on September 1, 1989, in Leipzig, the largest city in the state of Saxony, where the cathedral still rings with the works of Johann Sebastian Bach.

But it was in Loitsche, near Magdeburg, a dreary city of 200,000, that the Kaulitz parents chose to raise the boys in a typical middle-class home. Then, at the age of six, the twins' lives were turned upside down when their parents got divorced. A complete shock to the boys, they began to see the unfair world of adults in a new way, as they later expressed in the song "*Gegen Meinen Willen*" ("Against My Will") on *Schrei*. But their parents' separation also prompted Bill to start writing his first song lyrics and Tom to learn guitar seriously. It was also around this time that Bill had a revelation about his future destiny, while watching a TV show about Nena, a very popular German singer.

Nena became famous worldwide thanks to "*99 Luftballons*," which came out in 1983. Learning about her, young Bill saw her as an inspiration, and got the idea that his future destiny was to become a star like her! Who could have guessed that one day Nena, herself a mother of twins (Sakias and Larissa, born in 1990), would be on the same movie poster as Bill — in 2006 for *Arthur and the Invisibles*, the animated film by Luc Besson. In the German version, Nena dubs the voice of the Princess Selenia and Bill voices the lead role of Arthur.

After their parents' split, the Kaulitz children had a newly formed family, once their mother remarried rock guitarist Gordon Trümper. He encouraged the twins musically. Though Bill was not keen immediately, Tom threw himself into music wholeheartedly. Singing together the brothers' voices work well, and by the age of eight, they are already composing songs, one of which, "*Leb' die Sekunde*," would eventually appear up on *Schrei*, their first album. In 1998, before their 10th birthday, the twins sent their first demos, recorded on cassette, to several record companies, encouraged by the strong support from their mother and stepfather.

Having music as an outlet meant a great deal to Bill and Tom, especially since the boys were not thrilled with school, with its rules, discipline, conformity. . . . They rebelled against the system while still very young. Bill and Tom didn't look like their classmates, or have the same goals. Of course, their teachers didn't hesitate to point this out. The Kaulitz boys were eager to find a way out, and fast!

2001 marks a turning point in their life. Barely 12, they often had jam sessions for friends, in places that look more like deserted garages than clubs. Among the young fans, there was a drummer just a year older than them, a conservatory student named Gustav Klaus Wolfgang Schäfer. Blown away by the Kaulitz brothers, Gustav introduced them to one of his friends, Georg Moritz Hagen Listing, a bass guitarist, the oldest of the four. They bonded instantly and joined the group. The two new members shared the same passion for music as the twins. Gustav had played drums since the age of five, and was a big fan of Eric Clapton and Joe Cocker. Georg had been devoted to bass guitar since the age of 12, growing up listening to the Rolling Stones and AC/DC. They came up with a name for the band: Devilish. (Later on, when they signed with Sony in 2003, they renamed themselves Tokio Hotel.) The foundation of the band was set: a solid rock sound with insightful and heartfelt lyrics. And off they went for a series of mini-concerts in clubs in and around Magdeburg. Bill reminisces, "We were onstage almost every weekend, playing really often, and experiencing our very first sessions as a group."

And the wheel of fortune continued to turn: Bill entered the *Kinder-Star-Search* competition, the German version of *Star Search*. He may have missed first prize by a (spiked) hair, but all was not lost. Bill discovered that there is no doubt about it: he is meant to be onstage. His charisma charmed the crowd — especially producer Peter Hoffmann, who decided to go see one of the group's concerts in Magdeburg. Looking like an androgynous goth-rock elf, the singer couldn't help but further win Hoffmann over. On the strength of that show, Hoffmann then decided to take the quartet under his wing, and, to help him mould the young band, he enlisted renowned composers and lyricists Pat Benzner, Dave Roth, and David Jost, who, having collaborated with big names like Faith Hill and The Doors, helped Bill, Tom, Georg, and Gustav refine their sound.

And so Devilish became Tokio Hotel.

A girl should never ask us to choose between her and the group. She'll be disappointed because the group will always come first!
Bill

« In our band, everyone is free to do what he wants, but it's true that we all talk about it among ourselves and we each have our own opinion! »

"We have been very surprised by how quickly things have happened," Bill said. "What I mean is that Magdeburg is just a tiny little town and opportunities like this seem to happen thousands of miles away. However, we felt at home as soon as we walked into the studio. After the euphoria and excitement at the beginning, we immersed ourselves in working, spending all our free time and our holidays at the studio. We learned an incredible amount during this time and we became closer, not only as friends, but as a group."

Tokio Hotel is born. Why that name? Partly because it does not sound German, even though the spelling of the Japanese capital with an "i" instead of the "y" is certainly German. As Bill explains: "We were searching for a name that would characterize us as a group. We love all the big cities and wanted one that was dynamic but not that famous. We also wanted another symbol and hotel suited us because, at the time, we wanted to spend a lot of time in hotels. . . . That was a sign of success!"

Observers of the music scene — those who like to categorize musical groups into precise genres — were astonished at first by how crazy young girls were over these four uniquely styled young men. Early press coverage, both positive and negative, often compared Tokio Hotel to a new "boy band." Complete horror for Bill, Tom, Georg, and Gustav! In contrast to all those ultracommercial boy bands seemingly cast from the same mold, who were all the rage in the 1990s, the Magdeburg foursome demanded the status of artists right from the start. Never compromising, they play their own music, which they love more than anything. Very pro-fessional — "We all want to do our best and we want our songs to be perfect, to be able to communicate onstage all those wonderful times in the studio" — they believe they have started their own movement in the larger family of rock music. "I have fought against the boy band idea since we signed our first contract. I was very young but I didn't want us to have to change our music or our style," Bill maintains. Staying true to their vision worked out better than anyone could have imagined. Tokio Hotel's music, sung in the language of Goethe,

spreads outside the borders of Germany. Because language and lyrics are so key to people identifying with music, very few German artists have been able to break through to audiences who don't speak their language. Tokio Hotel has proven to be the exception to the rule.

Having known each other before their success and having climbed the steps of fame as a group, Tokio Hotel decided to live together in a large apartment in Hamburg. "It's very practical, and it's good for everyone," explains Georg, and Tom adds, "It's better than living at home and we don't have to get up early for school either!" It's pretty cool there even if Bill does monopolize the bathroom putting on his makeup! They eat junk food: pizza, hamburgers, milkshakes . . . "If you give us something [to eat that] we're not familiar with, forget it. We won't even try it!" In short, the life of a bachelor . . . and on the personal side, no one in the band had a really serious romantic relationship in their early years of success. Too much stress, too much moving around . . . and in particular, not enough free time. Which Bill admits freely: "It's true that with our lifestyle, it's very hard to have an established relationship, and our love songs are often inspired by stories we've heard. Personally, since the success of *Schrei* I've had several girlfriends, but nothing serious. That doesn't mean I don't still suffer from the breakups. Being in love does as much good as it does harm. . . ." Gustav confirms: "The group doesn't allow for a real love life. We're often away, or busy with our music." While Georg opened up about having a girlfriend in 2009, Tom, who dreams of meeting the Olsen twins, had his own two cents to add: "We can take advantage when we're on tour, because we each have our own hotel room! . . . Sometimes we might have a real connection with a fan during a concert, and if we meet afterwards, why not get better acquainted if we like each other?" Is he showing off a little? In any case, TH fans, consider yourselves warned . . . Tom's on the prowl.

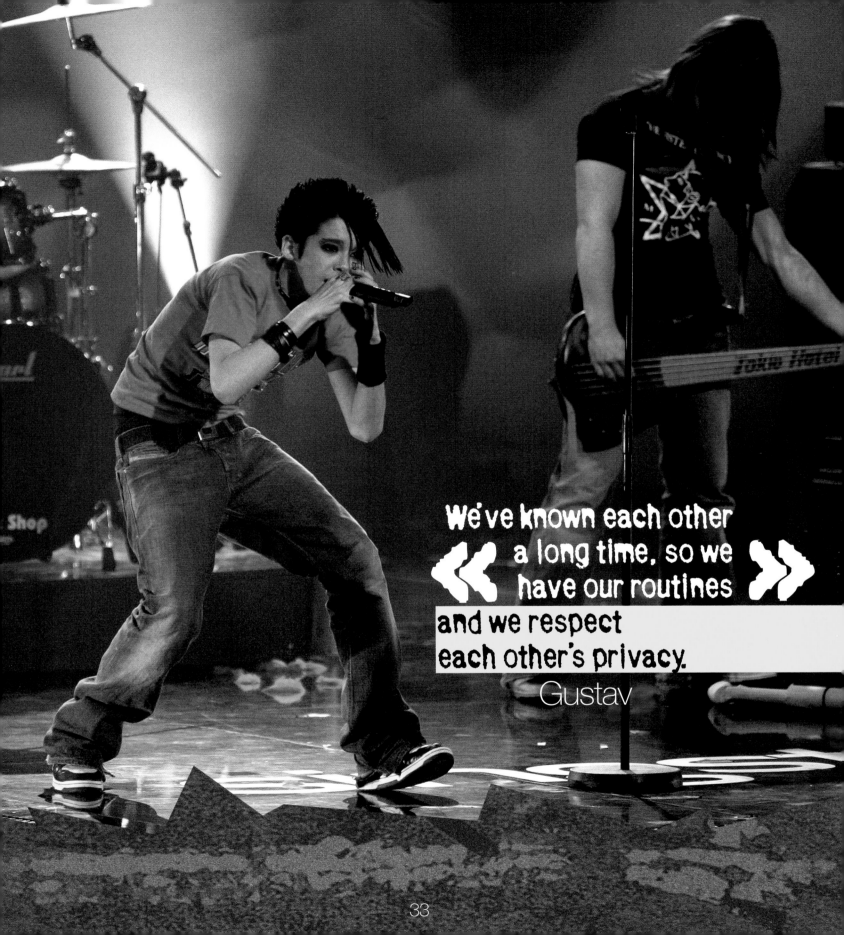

«We've known each other a long time, so we have our routines» and we respect each other's privacy.

Gustav

THROUGH THE MONSOON

2A

3

Behind the scenes of the video "Durch den Monsun." July 3, 2005, in the Berlin area, Tokio Hotel filmed the video that sent them to the top of the charts once more. Other than some bantering and coffee breaks, everyone got down to work like the pros they are.

"I'm fighting all this power coming in my way.
Let it take me straight to you.
I've been running night and day.
("*Durch den Monsun*," from *Schrei*)

9A   10

KATAPULT

GENERATION

I'm very stubborn.
I have to get
involved in
everything and I
hate it when people
tell me what to do.

BILL

last name : Kaulitz
first name : Bill
nickname : Macky
occupation : singer and songwriter
date of birth : September 1, 1989
astrological sign : Virgo
place of birth : Leipzig, Germany
height : 6' **weight :** 115 lbs **eye color :** brown
hair : spiky, dark blond dyed black
family : His parents, Simone and Jörg Kaulitz, got divorced when he was six. He was raised by his mother and stepfather Gordon Trümper, in Loitsche.
pets : a dog (Scotty) and a cat (Kasimir)
qualities : loyal, confident, dynamic
faults : stubborn, jealous
likes : partying; fashion and customizing his clothing; pizza; Coke; anything artistic
dislikes : wasps because he's allergic; spineless people; mathematics
distinguishing features : a tongue piercing which he got when he was 12; a right eyebrow piercing, obtained at 14; a tattoo of the group's logo on the nape of his neck; another star-shaped tattoo on his hip; *Freiheit 89* ("Freedom 89") on his arm, which he got on his 18th birthday; and one down his side which reads, "We'll never stop screaming," and "We're going back to the roots."
favorite artists : Green Day, David Bowie, Keane, Coldplay
favorite songs : "Nothing Else Matters" (Metallica), "Try Again" (Keane), "Boulevard of Broken Dreams" (Green Day)
his type of girl : Ashley Olsen, Angelina Jolie, Heidi Klum

GOTH MANGA IDOL

Multiple tattoos and piercings, polished nails, doe eyes, Pokemon hair . . . Bill, who plays up gender ambiguity, equally toys with the rules of fashion. He mixes a leather biker jacket, tightened up baggy jeans, and vintage running shoes with a ton of gothic accessories, like skull rings, studded belts, and ripped gloves. His mother, a dressmaker, introduced him to the art of customizing his own clothes. Since 2006, he has completely fallen for the T-shirt lines developed by Christian Audigier, Smet, and Ed Hardy, and said he'd one day love to design clothes himself.

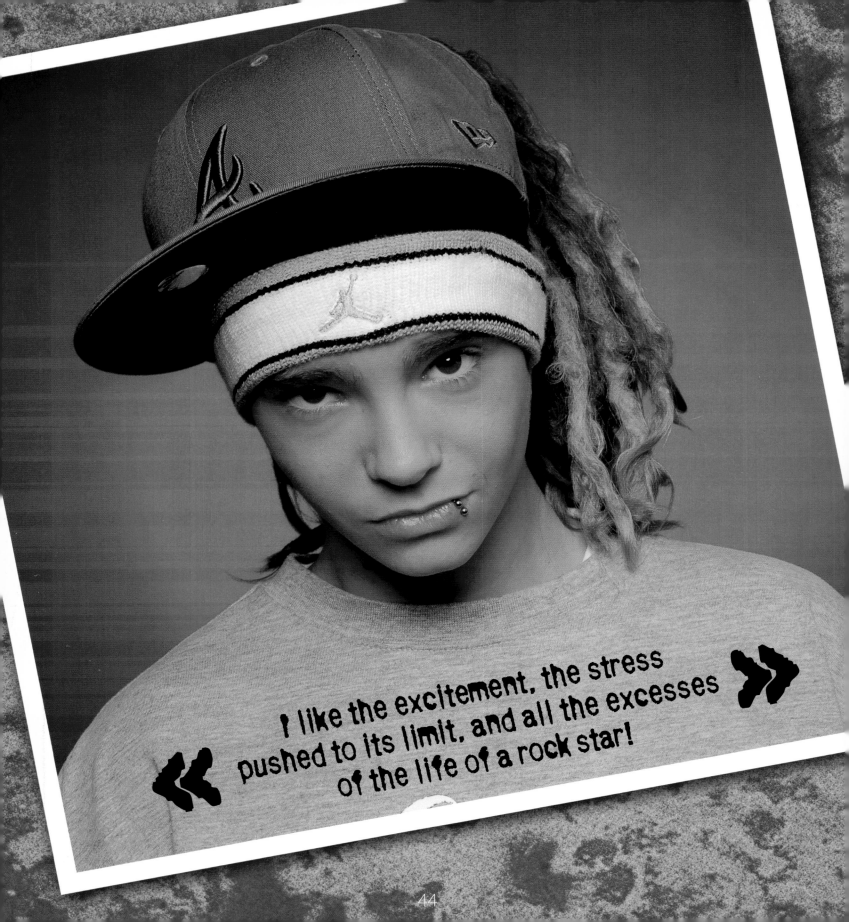

I like the excitement, the stress pushed to its limit, and all the excesses of the life of a rock star!

TOM

last name : Kaulitz
first name : Tom
occupation : guitarist and composer
date of birth :
September 1, 1989
astrological sign : Virgo
place of birth : Leipzig, Germany
height : 5'11"
weight : 115 lbs
hair : dark blond dreadlocks
eye color : brown
family : His parents, Simone and Jörg Kaulitz, got divorced when he was six. Like Bill, he was raised by his mother and stepfather Gordon Trümper, who gave him his first taste for music. The family lived in Loitsche, near Magdeburg. Tom was born 10 minutes before his twin brother.
pets : a dog (Scotty) and a cat (Kasimir)
qualities : approachable, good sense of humor, frankness
faults : flirtatious, spiteful, jealous
likes : girls, his gigantic guitar collection
dislikes : losing his laptop (he's addicted to it, like his brother), phony girls, routine, school
distinguishing features : a piercing on the left side of his lower lip, which he got when he was 14
favorite artists : Samy Deluxe, Snoop Dogg, Foo Fighters
his type of girl : Ashley Olsen, Angelina Jolie, Pamela Anderson, Jessica Alba

RAGGA STREET GUITAR

"I've been wearing dreadlocks since I was 11 and I would really feel naked without them. So, I think I'll keep them for a few more years. . . ." Tom began wearing his cool Rasta street look when he was quite young. With his trucker caps and scarves practically glued to his head, his long blond dreads fall onto his XXL T-shirts, which he wears with pants baggy enough for Biggie. In contrast to his brother, who likes to accentuate his skinny frame, Tom dresses like a rapper who could weigh almost 300 pounds.

My mother taught me to follow my instincts in life, even if it might mean failing.

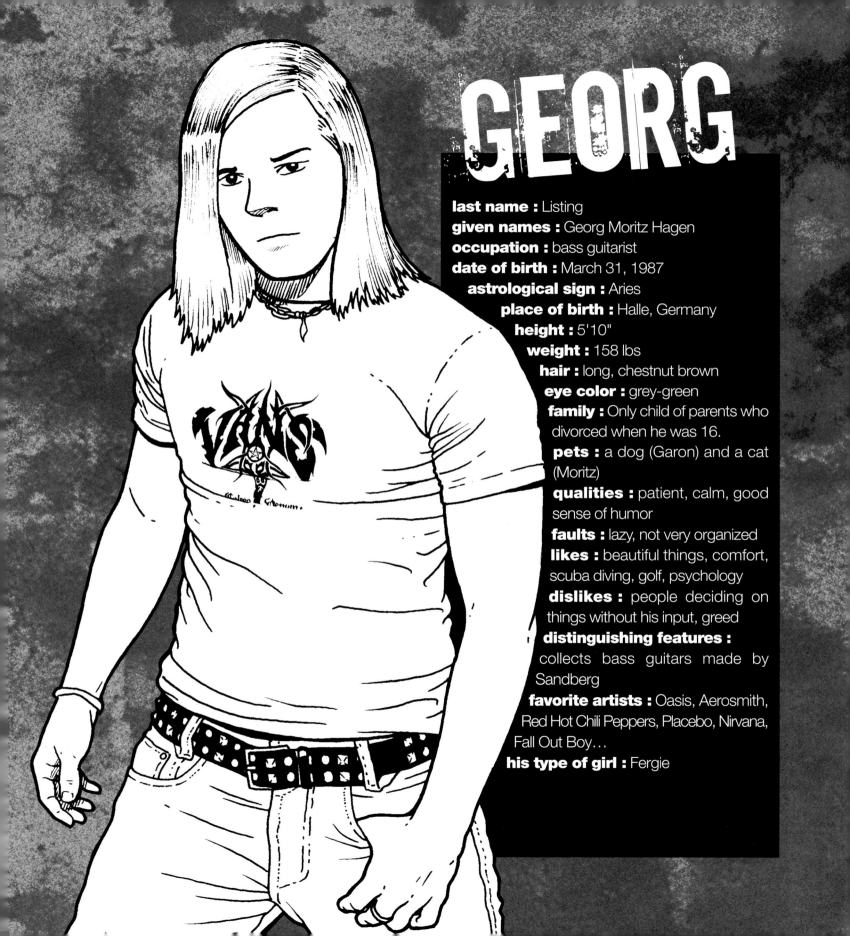

GEORG

last name : Listing
given names : Georg Moritz Hagen
occupation : bass guitarist
date of birth : March 31, 1987
astrological sign : Aries
place of birth : Halle, Germany
height : 5'10"
weight : 158 lbs
hair : long, chestnut brown
eye color : grey-green
family : Only child of parents who divorced when he was 16.
pets : a dog (Garon) and a cat (Moritz)
qualities : patient, calm, good sense of humor
faults : lazy, not very organized
likes : beautiful things, comfort, scuba diving, golf, psychology
dislikes : people deciding on things without his input, greed
distinguishing features : collects bass guitars made by Sandberg
favorite artists : Oasis, Aerosmith, Red Hot Chili Peppers, Placebo, Nirvana, Fall Out Boy…
his type of girl : Fergie

NEO-GRUNGE BASSIST

Like Gustav, the melancholy bassist with a clear gaze wears similar outfits from day to day. His special thing is his hair. Every morning, he spends at least half an hour smoothing it with a straightening iron, parting it precisely, and checking the length — it has to hit exactly at his shoulders. Once that's done, he slips on a T-shirt with the logo of one of his favorite rock groups, occasionally a neck chain, jeans, and running shoes. Georg, Bill, and Tom all have one passion in common besides music . . . long hair.

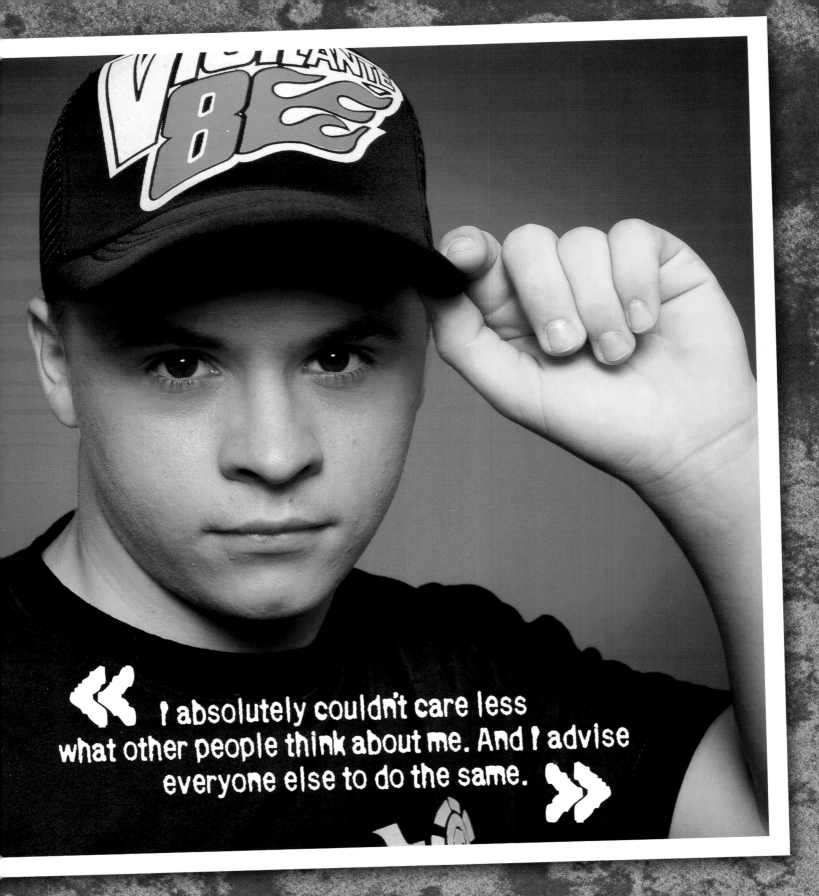

« I absolutely couldn't care less what other people think about me. And I advise everyone else to do the same. »

GUSTAV

last name : Schäfer

given names : Gustav Klaus Wolfgang

occupation : drummer

date of birth : September 8, 1988

astrological sign : Virgo

place of birth : Magdeburg, Germany

height : 5'7"

weight : 150 lbs

hair : short and blond

eye color : brown

family : His parents still live in Magdeburg, and he has a sister named Franziska.

qualities : sensitive, kind, a perfectionist

faults : very touchy, a bit too introverted

likes : listening to metal, mountain biking, sports, economics

dislikes : asparagus, critics

distinguishing features : He enjoys food and is a wonderful cook; he had a late growth spurt.

favorite artists : System of a Down, Metallica, Motörhead, Slipknot . . .

his type of girl : the one who will love him the way he is!

ENSITIVE HARD-ROCK DRUMMER

"I'm just a bit more reserved than the others and I avoid the limelight as much as possible." That's certainly true from his appearance. Shortly shorn hair, almost always covered with a baseball cap, plain T-shirt, jeans, and running shoes. That's Gustav's daily uniform! His only vanity was to replace his usual glasses with contact lenses for photo shoots, but started wearing his glasses in the promo shots for *Humanoid*. Self-conscious about his short height, the drummer does his best not to stand out. His bit of craziness? He loves to throw his T-shirt to the crowd at the end of a concert.

I'm not comfortable with
one-night stands. That type of relationship is
superficial and devoid of feeling. Bill

Tokio Hotel never anticipated that some of their most passionate fans outside their native Germany would hail from France. Frankly, we were the first to be surprised by how popular our songs were in France.

Bill

Bill : « We never thought we'd have such success in France, even in our wildest dreams!
I never thought we'd have so many fans there, who can actually sing our songs in German. That really surprised us and made us feel welcome! »

Tom : « We could see exactly when we became a sensation in France. It makes us happy to be well liked in a foreign country. »

Tom : « Bill and I like the same type of girl. But if we kissed the same girl for the first time, we'd never have a problem over a love affair. We're always in sync. »

Bill : « I don't have an ideal look that a girl should have. »

Hearts are pounding for Tokio Hotel in London, England, as well. Check out these TH fans who did their nails in imitation of Bill's. The girls were in a crowd waiting for the group to leave the O2 Academy Islington.

« The band doesn't allow for a real relationship. We're often away or busy with our music. Gustav »

As Tokio Hotel made their way through the Munich Olympiahalle, on April 24, 2007, the crowd became hysterical. People in the first rows lined up for hours before they got to their seats.

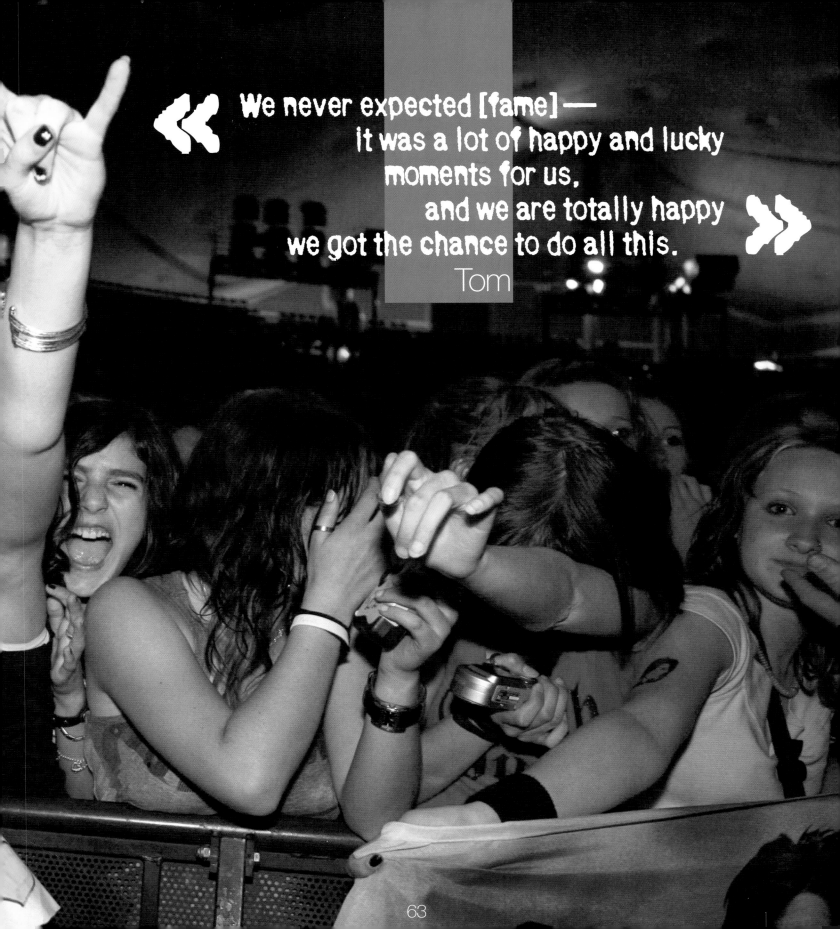

We never expected [fame]—it was a lot of happy and lucky moments for us, and we are totally happy we got the chance to do all this.
Tom

Tokio Hotel was a big favorite at the 16th Echo Awards, held March 25, 2007, and were welcomed by an impressive number of admirers.

On July 18, 2006, filming the video for "Der Letzte Tag" ("The Last Day"), Tokio Hotel took over the roof of the famous movie theater Kosmos in Berlin. Of course, the fans didn't miss a single instant. . . .

When French fans found out that their idols would be interviewed live on NRJ on March 20, 2007, they rushed en masse at dawn to the doors of the famous radio station. Fortunately, the band had a bit of time to sign autographs. . . .

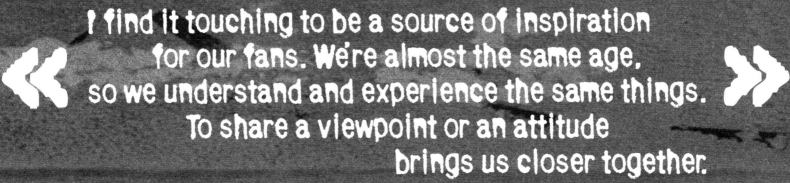

« I find it touching to be a source of inspiration for our fans. We're almost the same age, so we understand and experience the same things. To share a viewpoint or an attitude brings us closer together. »

Bill

DIZZYING
SUCCESS

December 1, 2005, in Munich. Less than two months after their first CD *Schrei* was released, Tokio Hotel receives the Best Pop National Act at the Bambi Awards. This prize, given to the most popular artist of the year, is determined by the German press group Hubert Burda Media. Created in 1948, the original prize was in porcelain. Since 1958, it's been made of gold.

September 6, 2006, Ludwigshafen, Germany. Tokio Hotel wins Best Group of the Year at the 26th Goldene Stimmgabel (which means "Golden Tuning Fork").

At the Dome, in Dusseldorf, April 28, 2007, Bravo Supershow awards the group with the Gold-Otto Superband Rock for the second year in a row. The band thanks the fans by singing "Spring Nicht ."

October 6, 2005. The group is recognized with the Comet, in the Best Newcomer category, at Oberhausen Arena, in Germany. This awards ceremony has been broadcast on Viva, a Berlin music channel, since 1995.

At the Eins Live Krone ceremony, December 7, 2006, in Bochum, organized by a German radio station, the band wins "Best German Group — Live" of the year.

We have the sensation of progressing by leaps and bounds. We never thought that this would get so big. . . .

Georg

> **With three songs, we've become the most popular German group. One could compare us to a boy band, but that would be a huge mistake. That's not our style. Bill**

The phenomenon had barely started before it grew exponentially. Number one, first in Germany, then in Austria, the band invaded Europe little by little, with only two albums. France, in particular, took to Tokio Hotel; out of two million copies produced, 500,000 were sold in France. Another sign of their huge success: tickets for the first 70,000 seats of their French tour in October sold out in barely two days. A record time for such a young group, who's now playing in the big leagues. The arrival of their album *Scream* in June 2007 — a compilation of their best songs recorded in English — marked their international mission: to spread Tokio Hotel fever around the world!

It all started in the summer of 2005. Their debut single "*Durch den Monsun*" went straight to the top of the charts and announced their first album *Schrei, so laut du kannst* ("Scream as loud as you can"), which came out at the beginning of the school year. In a few short weeks, *Schrei* took off and went gold in Germany and Austria. After their second single, "*Schrei*," came out, TH pandemonium hit: the album went double platinum in Germany, platinum in Austria, and gold in Switzerland. More than 100,000 copies were sold in France. At the same time, critical recognition poured in. At the prestigious Echo Awards, the quartet was nominated in the categories for Best National Pop Rock Group, Best National Newcomer, Best National Single of the Year, Best Video Production, and Best Producers for Hoffmann, Benzner, Roth, and Jost. At Munich in December, Tokio Hotel won the award for Best Pop National Act at the 2005 Bambi ceremony.

2006 was the year when Tokio Hotel established themselves irrevocably in the hearts of young European fans: tours, promotions, awards, dedications, videos, innumerable interviews, and a strong presence online. . . . The fever was rising. The fans were dying for their new release, *Zimmer 483*, which came out in April 2007. The album went straight to the top of the charts. On the 483 Tour, the band played to full house after full house. And the crowd was growing — from 6,000 fans on April 3 in Prague to more than 18,000 on May 14 in Cologne. In all, 22 concerts were sold out. After two sold-out shows in France, the fans demanded more concerts and Tokio Hotel decided to play 12 more there in October of that year. *Danke schön!*

May 22, 2006. Tokio Hotel wins the Bild Osgar in Leipzig, in the music category. For the last 13 years, this award has been given to people who advance Germany's cultural values.

March 25, 2007, in Berlin. At the Echo Music Awards, Tokio Hotel wins Best National Video for "Der Letzte Tag." The year before, they had won the Echo for Best National Newcomer.

May 3, 2007, in Cologne. The quartet steals the three coveted Comet awards in the categories Best Video ("Der letzte Tag"), Best Band, and the Super Comet for their body of work. They were nominated in four categories and were the big favorites of the evening.

"It was an amazing experience! I really enjoyed myself. The film was brilliant and Luc Besson is a fantastic guy who has made some great films. . . . I think it's an experience I'd like to try again, but only for good, interesting films . . ." In November 2006, in Paris, Bill attended the worldwide premiere of *Arthur et les Minimoys* (*Arthur and the Invisibles*), an animated film where the voice of the male hero is dubbed in French by a woman. For the German version, Bill voiced Arthur and he continued his role in promoting the film at the German premiere in Berlin on January 21. Debuting an even wilder haircut than usual, Bill was a sensation for the huge crowd of fans . . . and director Luc Besson. Bill and his character Arthur look like they may have the same hair stylist. . . .

EIN FILM VON LUC

KRAFTWERK

Creators of the electro-pop sound, Kraftwerk are responsible for giving rise to the music now synonymous with late nights dancing at clubs — strong beats, experimental rhythms, minimal lyrics, and a lot of help from the synthesizer. The group, whose name translates from German to power plant or station, came into being in 1970 when two young musicians from Dusseldorf, Florian Schneider and Ralf Hütter, met. Four years later two new members joined the group, Wolfgang Flur and Karl Bathos, and their first album, *Autobahn*, debuted to worldwide success. Their style reflects the vision they have of the Ruhr region, where they're from, known for its widespread industry, its concrete factories, and its modern technology. A source of inspiration both universal and futuristic, Kraftwerk's music is mechanical and testifies to the robotisation of man. Like Tokio Hotel, Kraftwerk strongly asserts its nationality: "We are composing in German, our native language, which is very mechanical, and we use that for the base of our music." Since 1975, with the album *Radio-Activity*, Kraftwerk has simultaneously recorded and released an English version of their music for their international audience. Their contribution to the history of music is considerable, still influencing many artists, from Depeche Mode to Missy Elliot, Daft Punk to Rammstein. . . .

SCORPIONS

Since German is pretty much only spoken in Germany, the group from Hanover chose the language of Shakespeare to express itself right from the start of its recording career with *Lonesome Crow*, its first album in 1972. The album took off, and the Scorpions were a worldwide phenomenon during the '70s with hard-rock hits like "No One Like You" and ballads such as "Still Loving You." The Scorpions are still a good example of musical success among young German groups. Known worldwide, thanks to monumental tours, they were particularly popular in Japan, where they recorded the *Tokyo Tapes* live in 1978. The four guys from Magdeburg, who grew up in the Scorpions' wake, were brought up listening to their strong, commercial sound, but took up the challenge of singing in their native language before expanding into English as well.

NENA

A huge idol in Germany and also popular worldwide, this extraordinary singer inspired Bill profoundly at a young age. It was while watching one of her broadcasts on television that he discovered his life's direction. Gabrielle Susanne Kerner — a.k.a. Nena — was born in Hagen in 1960. (Not to be confused with Nena Hagen, another famous German artist!) At the age of 21, she made her debut with the group Nena, best known for its international success "*99 Luftballons*." Three years later she tried out a solo career and since then has recorded several dozen albums, including a hit single in 2005, "*Liebe ist*" ("Love Is").

THE CURE

Adored by a whole generation of now-30-somethings, British rocker Robert Smith of The Cure came out of the post-punk movement, and is still an idol. Even younger fans think of him as the forerunner of his stark look. Heavy eyeliner, red lips, black wardrobe, disheveled hair, he opened the door to a whole new style, while the clean-cut look was still the rage. Bill is one of his many fans.

MAKE-UP ROCK

INDOCHINE PLACEBO

Bill also follows in the style footsteps of French new wave rockers Brian Molko and Nicola Sirkis of Indochine, who wear makeup, playing on the androgynous rock look. Known for this since 1981, Indochine's rise to popularity was in the wake of The Cure. Placebo continued the trend with the release of their first, self-titled album in 1996. At the age of 10, Bill decided to put on vampire makeup for Halloween, and it was a real discovery for him — his stage look was born.

PROPERTY OF BELLEVUE

GOD OF GLAM ROCK

DAVID BOWIE

"I don't know how many times I've watched his science-fiction movie *Labyrinth*. I think it's brilliant," declares Bill. In the 1986 feature film by Jim Henson, the man who brought us Ziggy Stardust becomes Jareth incarnate, king of the shaggy-haired goblins. (Not far off Bill's role in *Arthur and the Invisibles* . . .) Bowie, one of the originators of the "glam destroy" style, was ahead of his time, and inspired and encouraged a whole generation of artists, including Marilyn Manson (in his *Mechanical Animals* period). Another singer to emulate Bowie is Bill, who added just a touch of manga to his look . . .

THE WORLD
AT THEIR FEET

After conquering Germany, Switzerland, and Austria, the Tokio Hotel fever spread into the hearts of thousands of French fans, who, in just a few hours, bought up all the tickets for Zimmer 483 Live. The sold-out tour, anticipated for over six months, started in Clermont-Ferrand on October 10, 2007, and finished on the 29th at Toulon. The stunning success of this tour opened the door for the 20-plus dates of the 1000 European Hotels Tour starting early in 2008. While France was honored again, so were some Eastern European countries, as well as Sweden, Italy, and even Canada. . . . Nothing can stop the Tokio Hotel fever! After Israel, the next stop was the United States.

Hysteria Worthy
of the Beatles

Four and a half million albums sold worldwide, hundreds of thousands of DVDs, more than two hundred thousand products with their image. . . . The group is breaking all records for success and popularity, following the example of the Fab Four in the '60s. Raised to the level of international rock stars, these young artists live their dreams passionately and at a frenetic pace while managing their careers in an ultra-professional manner. An armada of technical teams, about 40 people, follows in the wake of Tokio Hotel's tours: translators, an appointed chef, and one person responsible solely for supplying Tom with the seven guitars that he "consumes" at each concert!

The last time I cried? . . . The few times we've had to cancel concerts because I was sick. I had no voice and I couldn't go onstage. From our dressing rooms, we could hear the fans chanting our name, while we waited for a miracle after the doctor's visit. Unfortunately, in that type of situation, it's better not to put strain on the vocal cords.

Bill

[Our fans] are really incredible and loud—we love it. They live this life with us. . . . One even named a star after us, so in outer space there's a star called Tokio Hotel. Bill

WELL-DESERVED VACATION...

In December 2007, after a year filled with more than 40 concerts, much traveling, the release of *Zimmer 483*, and a crazy day-to-day schedule, the Kaulitz twins finally scored a break — in the Maldives. There, on the unending white sand and in the crystalline waters of the Ari Atoll, the makeup, the stress, and the pandemonium disappeared. Time for surf shorts and chilling out! The only schedule during vacation? Sessions in the Jacuzzi, cocktails, swimming, tanning . . . Absolute bliss, far from recording studios, TV cameras, and their home country. About 5,000 miles away . . .

It was a necessary break in paradise that the two brothers would love to establish as a tradition. Even if they work side by side the *whole* year, they still want to hang out when they get away for rest and relaxation! Said Bill, "We are always together. We are like one person and like soul mates. We don't have to talk."

AND THE WINNER IS...

Saturday, January 26, 2008, in Cannes, at the legendary NRJ Music Awards, Tokio Hotel surfed the wave of its success by winning the most coveted award: Best International Band of the Year. The annual ceremony, equivalent to a rock 'n' roll high mass, was watched by more than 6.5 million people. Crowds of eager fans waited for Tokio Hotel in front of the Carlton Hotel, where the guys did a photo shoot for *Tele 7 Jours*.

Even when they first arrived for the awards show, as they drove to their hotel from the airport, they could feel the fever building up on La Croisette. As soon as Bill and the band walked the famous red carpet of the Palais des Festivals, there was no doubt anymore: Tokio Hotel was about to win the jackpot again! At the NRJ show, the band appeared onstage as it was covered in a blanket of fog, with Bill illuminated by the ghostly lights of Midem. The crowd went wild. Although the boys work to exhaustion, until they are burnt out and overwhelmed, it's all worth it in the transcendent moment onstage before their fans and the music world.

France has always brought us luck !

For us, to triumph at the NRJ Music Awards is like winning the Palme d'Or at Cannes.

COMING TO AMERICA

In 2007, Tokio Hotel released their first singles in North America, "Scream" and "Ready, Set, Go!", and began playing shows in America and Canada. It was as if they were at the start of their career all over again, said Tom. "It's definitely been a nice change because here we have our small gigs but then directly after this we are going on our European tour where things will be much bigger. But it's been a while since we've played in small clubs and it's a lot of fun." Just as in Germany and then the rest of Europe, North American fans went crazy for Bill, Tom, Georg, and Gustav. The boys' quick triumph in the U.S.A. culminated in winning the 2008 MTV Video Music Award for Best New Artist, beating out American stars like Miley Cyrus, Katy Perry, and Taylor Swift.

 I've always dreamed of driving people crazy!
Bill

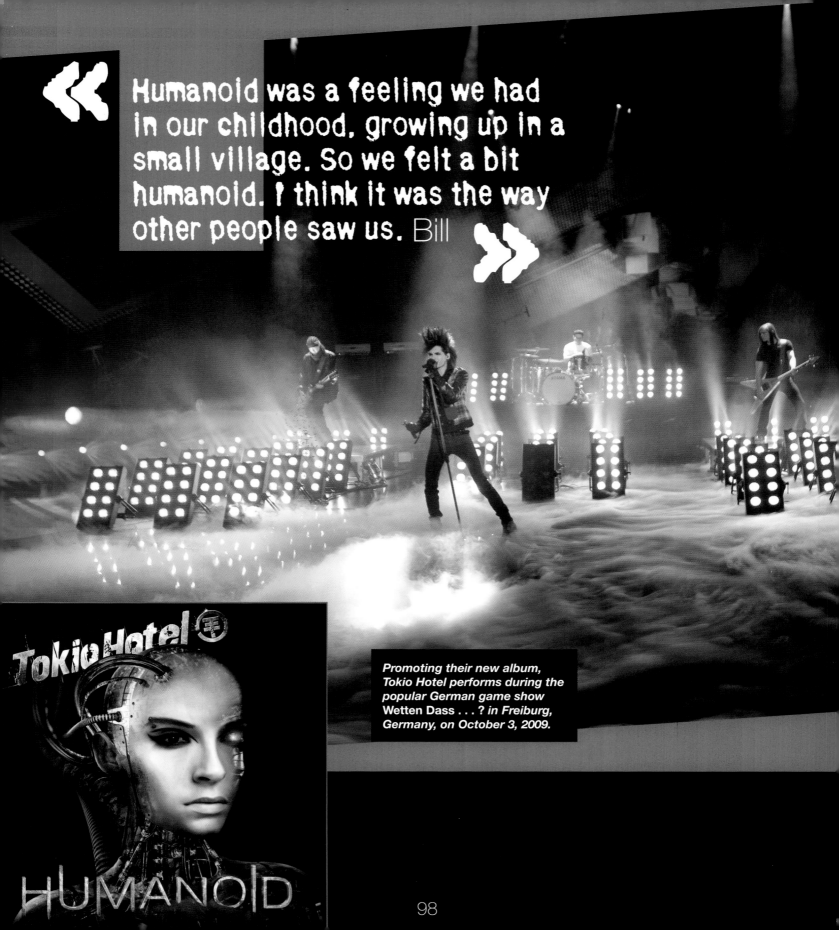

« Humanoid was a feeling we had in our childhood, growing up in a small village. So we felt a bit humanoid. I think it was the way other people saw us. Bill **»**

Promoting their new album, Tokio Hotel performs during the popular German game show Wetten Dass . . . ? in Freiburg, Germany, on October 3, 2009.

Tokio Hotel

HUMANOID

American fans were ecstatic when Tokio Hotel performed on the set of MTV's It's On with Alexa Chung at the Times Square Studios on October 19, 2009, in New York City.

TOKIO HOTEL

A for Automatic

After a long wait by patient fans, Tokio Hotel released their first single off *Humanoid* in September 2009. "Automatic"/"*Automatisch*" was accompanied by an ambitious video. Filmed in South Africa and directed by Craig Wessels, the science fiction–inspired video features the band members racing in muscle cars and performing in a futuristic junkyard inhabited by two robots who find a glimmer of romance with each other. "Shooting the 'Automatic' video three days in the desert was quite an adventure!" says Bill. "It was in the middle of nowhere in Africa — no cell phone reception, no Internet, not even paved roads. But in return we got a location that was just unreal. I've never had such a good feeling after leaving a set. I knew it was right from the beginning. When I first read the video script I knew this was exactly how I wanted to visualise our song 'Automatic.'"

B for Brothers

"We always know how the other one is feeling. I remember once I was out with my dad and I sensed that Bill wasn't feeling well. I made my dad call home and we found out that Bill had been taken to the hospital. It's always like that. We know what the other one is thinking and can finish each other's sentences," declares Tom.

C for Camouflage

Being world famous has its downsides. In order to go out somewhere incognito, the band has a fool-proof method, which Bill reveals: "There are two or three elements that are typical of our look and that's what allows everyone to recognize us. As soon as we change those little things, it's easy to go unnoticed. For example, all Tom has to do is hide his dreadlocks, wear a pair of glasses, and put on some tight pants, to be left alone."

FROM TO TO TO

D as in Devilish

Tokio Hotel started with a clean slate! Pre-adolescent lyrics, music too similar to other groups . . . Exit the "Devilish" style from their first years together. Or as Gustav puts it: "The other Devilish songs [apart from "*Leb' die Sekunde*," which they play live] are frankly too lame. We would be ashamed to play those onstage! Or we'd have to make new arrangements, but we'd have to make so many changes that it would almost be like writing a new song."

E as in Enemies

There have been so many new experiences for Tokio Hotel: huge popularity, concerts selling out so quickly, so many rock fans actually listening to German lyrics . . . and so many enemies in a very short time. Why such hatred? Those who dislike them and call them "Tokio Poubelle" (poubelle means garbage in French) and are ruthless on the Internet and even outside concerts. They've even shown up with nasty banners and stink bombs! Not exactly a rock 'n' roll attitude. . . .

What do the objects of this hatred have to say about it? "I've seen the blogs against us. I love to read them; they give me a good laugh. Mostly, they write stuff like we're just a boy band and that Bill is a homosexual. They don't shoot very high, and personally, that kind of criticism doesn't bother me," declares Tom, backed by Bill. "We couldn't care less what people write on the Internet. If we worried about all the stupidity that's written about us, we'd go crazy." Bill adds, "What's most shocking is the violent behavior between different groups of fans [in Europe]. It's getting worse than soccer and frankly, it makes us very uncomfortable. We're there to make music and entertain, not to have people beating each other up."

F for Fan Fanaticism

So much success brings run-ins with fans: pulled hair, ripped T-shirts, screaming, and crying. While most of their fans are just overwhelmed by meeting their idols, some are very emotional, and sometimes psychologically fragile. For fans struggling with depression, they wrote "*Spring nicht*"/ "*Don't Jump*" to say that suicide is not the solution. Of their music in general, Bill says, "We want our fans to identify with it, to find themselves in our music. I write about our lives and things we experience or things that happen to our friends and fans. They write us a lot and tell us about their lives, that inspires us as well. . . . We're trying to live our dreams and not to give up, expressing ourselves no matter what people may say."

G for Goth

A fan of Brian Molko, the singer from Placebo, Bill loves wearing bold eye makeup, even though he's not into the Goth movement or black romanticism. But with his black and red wardrobe, his nail polish and his tattoos, his overall appearance is very dark and many people mistake his personal style for a Goth. Bill does share one influence with Goth culture: horror films. "As a kid I loved all the vampire movies, so that might be an influence [on my style]."

H for Humanoid

After a long break between albums, Tokio Hotel was back and better than ever with the release of *Humanoid* in October 2009. Again the band worked with producer David Jost but, says Jost, "For the first time, Bill and Tom have co-produced a majority of the tracks on the new album. . . . Bill and Tom had a very clear vision of how the tracks should sound production-wise in the end."

I for Ink

Stars, wings, swords, meaningful words, the TH logo. . . . The guys in Tokio Hotel are no strangers to getting inked. Said Gustav when he got his first tattoo and showed it to his bandmates, "They really like it. Bill has gone through the pain himself. He immediately took a good look at it. Only Tom warned me, 'Man, you know that will never come off?!'"

J for Japan

Incredible but true: when they chose their stage name, the band had never stepped foot in a Tokyo hotel. Said Bill of the Japanese capital, "It's like a huge city and of course it's a cool sound; 'Tokyo' sounds so cool. So that was the main reason why we chose it." While they haven't played in Tokyo, Tokio Hotel recorded "*Monsun o koete*," the Japanese version of "Monsoon."

K for Karate

Tom tried this martial art but ended up quitting because his companions made fun of his dreadlocks and even grabbed them to help knock him over. . . . Not fair!

L for Love

Very busy with their music, tours, promotions,

recordings, and interviews, the foursome find it hard to have a proper relationship. While Tom does not hesitate to brag about his conquests, Bill is much more reserved on the subject. As for Georg, Tom gave the best advice, "If you run into Georg, don't wait to take the first step, because he never will!" Georg told *Bravo* magazine that he met a girl at a party in Magdeburg in early 2009; who knows who made the first move, but they've been together since and are very much in love!

M for Madame Tussauds

In 2008, Bill was immortalized in wax at the Berlin Madame Tussauds Museum. Fans came out in droves to see the Bill replica, and some got a little frisky, kissing and grabbing it!

N for Nokia

For the first time in their careers, the band agreed to a deal with Nokia, promoting the company through an exclusive acoustic concert on August 27, 2009, in Cologne, Germany. Fans traveled from Finland, Italy, and even Mexico to see the band perform a preview show of *Humanoid*.

O for Online

Tokio Hotel loves keeping in touch with their fans through their website, blog posts, and personal videos. "The Internet is really important and has been great for us," says Tom. "It's actually where people from other countries discover us and become fans. That's how we connected with fans all over the world. Then we go to their countries, play shows there, and meet them for the first time in person."

P for Producers

For the first time, Tokio Hotel recorded and produced some songs in America, working with The Matrix, who has worked with artists like Britney Spears, Katy Perry, and Korn. Describing songs on *Humanoid* as "strong, anthem-y" with "lots of guitars," The Matrix said, "The music business really needs Tokio Hotel right now. They're reviving that image of what a rock star is. . . . It doesn't sound like anything else out there right now. People don't want to hear a bunch of 808s and Auto-Tuned vocals. They want the real stuff."

Q as in Quartet

"We've known each other so long that we practically know everything about one another. We trust each other and nobody in the group would break a confidence of someone else's."

R for Rider

Like any musical act, Tokio Hotel has a list of requests, called a rider, which is given to venues in advance of a performance. And like any superstar musical act, there are rumors about the demands listed on Tokio Hotel's. Bullet-proof limousines? A 150-member security team? Requests that hallways be cleared outside their dressing rooms? Who knows what the band *actually* requires from a venue, and what is just rumor.

S for Surgery

In the middle of their European tour in March 2008, Tokio Hotel had to bring it to an abrupt end. After singing night after night, Bill had strained his vocal chords, and the doctors found a cyst on his larynx, which had to be removed surgically. While it was scary — both for Bill and his devoted fans! — the singer completely recovered, and canceled performances were the only damage done.

T for Translation

"Our lyrics are really important to us and we want everybody to understand them," says Bill. "When a lot of people from different countries started to pick up our music, we thought we should do an English version of chosen songs from our two German albums." Being a perfectionist, Bill made sure his words carried the same meaning in English even when direct translations didn't work. "Our German phrases like, 'big cinema,' it's '*grosses Kino*' in German. This red carpet is *grosses Kino*. It's like, 'beautiful,' 'awesome.'"

U for U.S.A.

"America is a huge professional fantasy; a kind of ultimate goal. But it's way too soon to talk about it," said Tom prudently before the band's first time stateside. The four decided to travel there anyway, in the summer of 2007, and were able to walk around in public without being recognized. Cut to two years later and their legions of American fans recognize them in an instant.

V for VMAs

MTV has been a big supporter of Tokio Hotel, and in 2008 the band was up for Best Pop

Video for "Ready, Set, Go!" and they won the coveted Best New Artist Moonman. Said Bill, "I think it's really, really special for us — it's America and it's our first American award, and that's so huge." The boys made a splash by arriving at the red carpet in a monster truck.

W for Wilcommen!

Since their first English album, Tokio Hotel has gained fans around the globe. Says Bill, "We want to play a world tour, that's kind of a dream for us." And a dream for TH fans, who would welcome the band to their country with open arms.

X as in Xtreme

It takes Bill at least half an hour to get his hair just right with a lot of help from Xtreme hair-spray and hair gel by Kyrell. It's not easy to achieve Bill's look!

Y as in Yoga

Once a concert is over, the band requests 40 minutes of peace and quiet to regain their "Zen" and relieve some stress. Their method? A mixture of slow breathing and relaxation exercises combined with authentic yoga.

Z as in Zimmer 483

Bill tells the story of this famous room: "483 is the number of the house we lived in on vacation in Spain. It's important to us because that's where we started to write the album. The atmosphere was special and the album expresses it very well."

TokioHotel
ZIMMER
483

TokioHotel
SPRING NICHT
Robots to Mars Remix

TokioHotel
DIE NEUE SINGLE!

TokioHotel
Schrei
so laut du kannst

TokioHotel
SCREAM

DISCOGRAPHY

Devilish Period
1. Lebe die Sekunde
2. It's so Hard to Live
3. I Needn't You
4. Schwerelos
5. Nothing's Like Before
6. Nichts wird besse
7. Schönes Mädchen aus dem All

• 2005 •

Schrei
Released in Germany,
September 19, 2005 – Island
1. Schrei
2. Durch den Monsun
3. Leb' die Sekunde
4. Rette mich
5. Freunde bleiben
6. Ich bin nicht ich
7. Wenn nichts mehr geht
8. Lass uns hier raus
9. Gegen meinen Willen
10. Jung und nicht mehr
    jugendfrei
11. Der letzte Tag
12. Unendlichkeit

• 2006 •

Schrei so laut du kannst
Released on March 24 in Germany, Austria, Switzerland, and Poland; April 17 in the Czech Republic and Slovakia; May 12 in The Netherlands; May 15 in Spain; and September 18 in France – Universal
1. Schrei
2. Durch den Monsun

3. Leb' die Sekunde
4. Rette mich
5. Freunde bleiben
6. Ich bin nich' ich
7. Wenn nichts mehr geht
8. Lass uns hier raus
9. Gegen meinen Willen
10. Jung und nicht mehr
    jugendfrei
11. Der letzte Tag
12. Unendlichkeit
13. Beichte
14. Schwarz
15. Thema Nr. 1
16. Schrei – Acoustic version
17. Durch den Monsun –
    Unplugged version

Rette mich
CD single released March 10, 2006 – Universal
1. Rette mich – video version
2. Rette mich – acoustic version
3. Thema Nr.1 – Demo 2003
4. Durch den Monsun – live video
5. Rette mich – video

Rette mich
Double CD released August 25, 2006 – Universal
CD 1
1. Der letzte Tag – single version
2. Der letzte Tag – Grizzly remix
3. Frei im freien Fall
4. Wir schliessen uns ein
5. Wir schliessen uns ein – video
CD 2
1. Der letzte Tag – single version
2. Der letzte Tag – acoustic
   version
3. Der letzte Tag – video
4. Tokio Hotel Gallery "Der letzte
   Tag"
5. Der letzte Tag – live

• 2007 •

Zimmer 483
Released February 26, 2007 – Universal
1. In die Nacht (title hidden)
2. Übers Ende der Welt
3. Totgeliebt
4. Spring Nicht
5. Heilig
6. Wo sind eure Hände
7. Stich ins Glück
8. Ich brech aus
9. Reden
10. Nach dir kommt nichts
11. Wir sterben niemals aus
12. Vergessene Kinder
13. An deiner Seite (Ich bin da)

Scream
Released June 1, 2007 – Universal
1. Scream: Schrei
2. Ready, Set, Go: Übers Ende
   der Welt
3. Monsoon: Durch den Monsun
4. Love Is Dead: Totgeliebt
5. Don't Jump: Spring Nicht
6. On the Edge: Stich ins Glück
7. Sacred: Heilig
8. Break Away: Ich brech aus
9. Rescue Me: Rette mich
10. Final Day: Der letzte Tag
11. Forgotten Children:
    Vergenessene Kinder
12. By Your Side: Ich bin da

Spring nicht
Released August 27, 2007
CD Single
1. Spring Nicht – album version
2. Spring Nicht – orchestral
   version
3. In Die Nacht
4. Outtakes – studio, a capella
5. Spring nicht – photo gallery

and making-of
DVD single
1. Spring nicht – video
2. Spring nicht – making of video
3. Stich ins Glück – unplugged
   video
4. Wir sterben niemals aus –
   unplugged video
5. Guided tour of the studio with
   Bill

• 2008 •

An deiner Seite (Ich bin da)
CD single released January 28, 2008 – Polydor
1. An deiner Seite (Ich bin da) –
   radio edit
2. 1,000 Meere – single version
3. Geh
4. An deiner seite (Ich bin da) –
   live
5. Scream – live in Bercy

• 2009 •

Humanoid
Released October 2 in Germany; October 6 in North America – Universal
1. Noise
2. Darkside of the Sun
3. Automatic
4. World Behind My Wall
5. Humanoid
6. Forever Now
7. Pain of Love
8. Dogs Unleashed
9. Human Connect to Human
10. Love & Death
11. Hey You
12. Zoom Into Me

VIDEOGRAPHY

• 2006 •
Schrei – Live

Released April 7, 2006, in Germany; January 2, 2007 in France – Universal

1. Jung und nicht mehr jugenfrei
2. Beichte
3. Ich bin nicht ich
4. Schrei
5. Leb' die Sekunde
6. Schwarz
7. Laß uns hier raus
8. Gegen meinen Willen
9. Durch den Monsun
10. Thema Nr.1
11. Wenn nichts mehr geht
12. Rette mich
13. Freunde bleiben
14. Der letzte Tag

+ Frei im freien Fall
  Unendlichkeit
  Durch den Monsun

+ Extras : One Night In Tokio

+ Picture gallery

• 2007 •
Leb die Sekunde
Behind the Scenes

Released January 2, 2007 – Universal

1. Jung und nicht mehr jugendfrei:

Der Anfang – bewegt/festge- halten
2. Schrei: Live – Stars for Free/Tag der deutschen Einheit
3. Freunde bleiben: Interview/Making Of "Schrei"
4. Durch den Monsun: Eure 20 Fanfragen
5. Unendlichkeit: The Dome/Comet
6. Lass un shier raus: Picture gallery
7. Vidéos: Durch den Monsun, Schrei

• 2007 •
Zimmer 483
Live in Europe

Released September 28, 2007 – Universal

1. Ubers Ende der Welt
2. Reden
3. Ich brech aus
4. Spring nicht
5. Der letzte Tag
6. Wo sind eure Hände
7. Durch den Monsun
8. Wir sterben niemals aus
9. Stich ins Glück
10. Ich bin nicht ich

11. Schrei
12. Vergessene Kinder
13. Leb' die Sekunde
14. Heilig
15. Totgeliebt
16. In die Nacht
17. Rette mich
18. An deiner Seite

• 2008 •
Tokio Hotel
TV
Caught on Camera!

Released December 9, 2008 – Universal

1. Intro
2. Tel Aviv, Paris, Cannes, Essen
3. TH-TV: MTV Europe Music Awards 2007
4. Montreal, Toronto, Los Angeles
5. TH-TV: Climbing with Gustav and Georg
6. New York City
7. TH-TV: On the Kart Track with Tom, Gustav, and Georg
8. New York City, Oberhausen
9. TH-TV: Hot Topics @ Hot Topic
10. TH-TV: Interview above the clouds
11. Lissabon, Paris
12. TH-TV: Shopping with Bill
13. Modena, Genf
14. Werchter, Mexico City
15. TH-TV: MTV VMA 2008: Music, Mayhem, Tokio Hotel

Leb die Sekunde
Behind the scenes
Tokio Hotel
BATACLAN PARIS
LE BATACLAN 75011 PARIS
NOUS PRODUCTIONS
(2-142638 & 3-142639) PRESENTE
TOKIO HOTEL
DIMANCHE 26 NOVEMBRE 2006
DEBOUT PLACEMENT LIBR
Prix uniqu
Prix TTC : EUR 28,60
(28,60EUR)
Frais de location inclus
Tokio Hotel
Schrei - Live
including subtitles in:
english français castellano polski 日本語 pycc
Leb die Sekunde
Behind the scenes
Tokio Hotel